15-Second Recipes:
A Cookbook
for Busy People

By Brendan Leonard

CONTENTS

1. Fistful of Potato Chips

2. Several Bites Out of
a Block of Cheese

3. String Cheese, One Bite

4. Hit(s) From a Can of Easy Cheese

5. Several Bites Out of a Block of
Cheese, But Also Put Some Crackers
in Your Mouth and Chew Them at
the Same Time

6. Smoothie That You Convinced
Someone Else to Make for You

7. Banana or Other Handheld Fruit

8. Several Spoonfuls From a
Container of Ice Cream

9. Deconstructed Cereal

10. Big Spoonful of Peanut Butter

11. Big Spoonful of Peanut Butter
Plus a Big Spoonful of Jelly

12. 10-Second Cheese Sandwich

13. Chocolate Chip Drink

14. Cold Soup in a Coffee Mug

15. Half of Someone Else's Sandwich

16. Uncooked Ramen

17. Ketchup Sandwich

18. Gummy Vitamin

19. Cows in a Blanket

20. Roommate's Leftovers

21. Exercise Food

22. Unused Condiment Packets from Past Takeout Orders

23. Cold Taco

24. Corn Dog Popsicle

25. Tortilla Chips from Bottom of Bag Poured Into a Jar of Salsa and Eaten With a Spoon

You're busy. You barely have time to eat, let alone cook some complicated meal involving pans and four or more ingredients and all kinds of crazy stuff like that.

Well, here's a collection of recipes for busy people like yourself. You can prepare all of these in 15 seconds or less. I guess none of them are really warmer than room temperature, so if that's not your thing, maybe look for a different cookbook, or try going to a restaurant, such as Arby's.

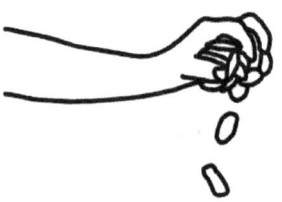

1
FISTFUL OF POTATO CHIPS

Serves: 1

Time: 3-5 seconds

Directions: Find a bag of potato chips somewhere in your dwelling, stick your hand into the bag, and grab as many chips as you can in one handful.

Optional: Eat the whole bag.

2
SEVERAL BITES OUT OF A BLOCK OF CHEESE

Serves: 1

Time: 10-15 seconds

Directions: Just take the wrapper off the cheese and start eating it like you would a big candy bar, but made of cheese. Pretty straightforward.

3
STRING CHEESE, ONE BITE

Serves: 1

Time: 5-15 seconds

Directions: Sure, you can actually string out the cheese if you have like nothing else to do today. But you're busy, so stick one end of the cheese stick into your mouth, push it against the inside of your cheek, and bend the other end so the whole thing fits in your mouth. There you go.

4
HIT(S) FROM A CAN
OF EASY CHEESE

Serves: 1

Time: 3-15 seconds

Directions: This is like a whippit, but instead of inhaling nitrous oxide, you get a cheese product in your mouth, so, nutritious, kind of.

5
SEVERAL BITES OUT OF A BLOCK OF CHEESE, BUT ALSO PUT SOME CRACKERS IN YOUR MOUTH TOO AND CHEW THEM AT THE SAME TIME

Serves: 1

Time: 15 seconds

Directions: The title here is intended to be self-explanatory.

6
SMOOTHIE THAT YOU CONVINCED SOMEONE ELSE TO MAKE FOR YOU

Serves: 1

Time: 5 seconds

Directions: Smoothies are delicious, refreshing, and often nutritious. But they're kind of a lot of effort. Fortunately, if you live with another human such as a spouse, child, parent, or butler, you can enjoy one without taking the time out of your schedule to gather ingredients and blend them up. Or, if you catch them at the right time, you might be able to convince the UPS driver to make one (obviously tell them they can have half).

7
BANANA OR OTHER HANDHELD FRUIT

Serves: 1-2

Time: 5-10 seconds

Directions: Not to point out the obvious, but many fresh fruits are pretty much ready to eat. Maybe avoid things like watermelon, pineapple, and pomegranates, which take way longer than 15 seconds to get to the edible part. Just usually wash it first.

8
SEVERAL SPOONFULS FROM A CONTAINER OF ICE CREAM

Serves: 1

Time: 15 seconds

Directions: For this recipe, you'll need a spoon of any size, and a container of ice cream, also of any size. Should be pretty obvious from there, I guess.

DECONSTRUCTED CEREAL

Serves: 1

Time: 8 seconds

Directions: Open a box of cereal and shove your hand into it. Bring a palmful of cereal to your mouth and shove cereal into your mouth.

Optional: Grab a vessel of milk or nondairy milk and drink straight from it after each mouthful of cereal.

10
BIG SPOONFUL OF PEANUT BUTTER

Serves: 1

Time: 6 seconds

Directions: Grab a jar of peanut butter, then find the biggest spoon you own that will fit into the peanut butter jar. Spoon out a gob of peanut butter and eat it off the big spoon.

*small spoons are fine too, but then I guess you just gotta do way more spoonfuls.

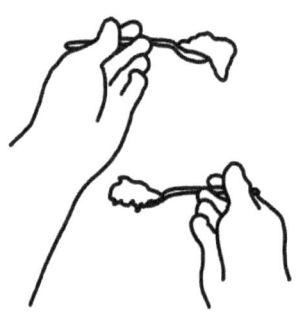

11
BIG SPOONFUL OF PEANUT BUTTER PLUS A BIG SPOONFUL OF JELLY

Serves: 1

Time: 12 seconds

Directions: I mean, if you want to get fancy, and you have time, the sky's the limit, really.

①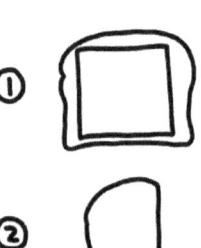

②

12
10-SECOND CHEESE SANDWICH

Serves: 1

Time: 10 seconds

Directions: Get a slice of bread, get a slice of deli cheese. Place the slice of deli cheese on the bread, then fold the bread in half, with the cheese in the middle. Boom there's your cheese sandwich.

13
CHOCOLATE CHIP DRINK

Serves: 1

Time: 5 seconds

Directions: If you or someone in your house bakes things every once in a while, there's a good chance you have chocolate chips somewhere in your kitchen cupboards. Find the bag, open it, bring the opening to your mouth, and pour chocolate chips in until your mouth is full.

Optional: Dark chocolate chips are technically healthier, allegedly.

COLD SOUP IN A COFFEE MUG

Serves: 1

Time: 15 seconds

Directions: Use a can opener to open soup can, unless it's one of those fancy cans with the pull tab thing. Pour soup into coffee mug. Drink soup.

THEIRS   YOURS

15
HALF OF SOMEONE ELSE'S SANDWICH

Serves: 1

Time: 5 seconds

Directions: This one is dependent on someone else near you making, or at least possessing, a sandwich. When you have verified that someone near you is eating a sandwich, simply ask them if you can have half of their sandwich.

16
UNCOOKED RAMEN

Serves: 1

Time: 3 seconds

Directions: Open packet of ramen noodles. Take bites of the cake of hard noodles, the same way you would a granola bar.

Optional: Pour a small amount of seasoning from the seasoning packet into your mouth with each bite of noodles.

(Submitted by: Anna Brones)

①

②

17
KETCHUP SANDWICH

Serves: 1

Time: 15 seconds

Directions: Grab a slice of bread and a squeeze bottle of ketchup. Coat one side of the bread with the desired amount of ketchup. Fold the bread in half. Ketchup sandwich.

Note: This recipe is not possible with glass bottles of ketchup. It is, however, possible with mustard.

18
GUMMY VITAMIN

Serves: 1

Time: 5 seconds

Directions: I guess you're not really supposed to eat more than one of these at a time, according to doctors, but they're pretty tasty.

①

②

19
COWS IN A BLANKET

Serves: 1

Time: 6-8 seconds

Directions: Grab a stick of string cheese and a slice of deli cheese. Wrap the deli cheese around the string cheese and begin eating.

(Submitted by Forest Woodward)

ROOMMATE'S LEFTOVERS

Serves: 1-2

Time: 10 seconds

Directions: (This recipe is dependent on having one or more roommates, who may be roommates, romantic partners, or your kids or parents.) To make Roommate's Leftovers, find a container of food that your roommate ate part of but not all of sometime in the preceding days. Pull it out and eat as much as you need to, without asking their permission, which would take more than 15 seconds. If you're feeling generous when you're done, offer your roommate some of the food.

21
EXERCISE FOOD

Serves: 1

Time: 6-8 seconds

Directions: If you exercise, you might have some specific foods you eat pretty much only when you're at the gym, or hiking, or riding your bicycle. When you're busy, which is always, these foods are fair game any time of the day, because they contain calories, and you need calories, fast.

22
UNUSED CONDIMENT PACKETS FROM PAST TAKEOUT ORDERS

Serves: 1

Time: 4-5 seconds

Directions: Honestly there aren't too many calories in takeout condiments (besides mayonnaise), but they are technically food, and maybe you have some laying around in a drawer or something?

23
COLD TACO

Serves: 1

Time: 15 seconds

Directions: Take a tortilla in one hand, and place a slice or block of cheese, or really anything that doesn't require spreading with a utensil, in the tortilla.

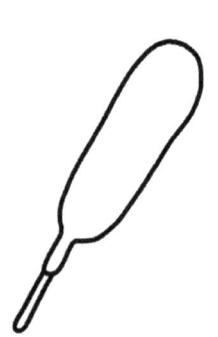

CORN DOG POPSICLE

Serves: 1

Time: 5 seconds

Directions: You're supposed to cook hot dogs before you eat them because although they're cooked, they can develop listeria. Corn dogs, however, are frozen, so therefore—Actually, sorry, I just looked this up on the internet. Don't eat corn dogs without cooking them. Just cross out this page, sorry again.

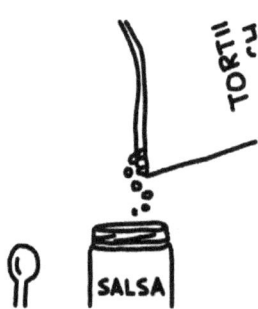

25
TORTILLA CHIPS FROM BOTTOM OF BAG POURED INTO JAR OF SALSA AND EATEN WITH A SPOON

Serves: 1

Time: 15 seconds

Directions: This is pretty elaborate and kind of requires a specific ratio of chips to salsa, but when you nail it, you will probably congratulate yourself, and also maybe hope no one sees you standing there, leaning over the sink, unprepared to explain what you're doing.

ABOUT THE AUTHOR

Brendan Leonard actually knows
how to cook, and quite enjoys it.
He just gets busy sometimes.
Find more of his work
at Semi-Rad.com.